This book is

my wonderful Husband Chris Browne and our Children Joshua and Becca. To my sisters Marilyn Cooper Bellamy and Irma Cooper. They had all encouraged me to reach my dreams.

Love, Isabelle Cooper-Browne- Author

Aa

A a
Aaron
apple

Bb

B b

Barb

Cc

C
My fat Cat
Cathy
c
Cat

Dd

D d

doughnut

Ee

E

Eva

e

eyes

Ff

F f

Gg

G g

Hh

H

Heather

h

house

Ii

I i

Isaiah

ice cream

Jj

J j

Jackie

jacket

Kk

K k
Katie
kites

Ll

L l

Lucy

lemons

Mm

M m

Marilyn

Nn

N n

Norman

nuts

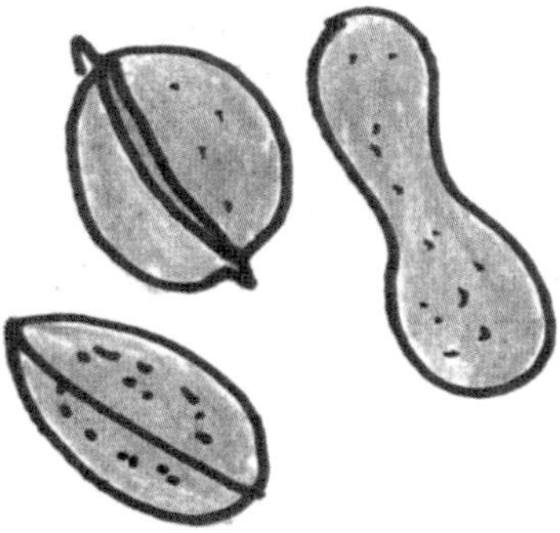

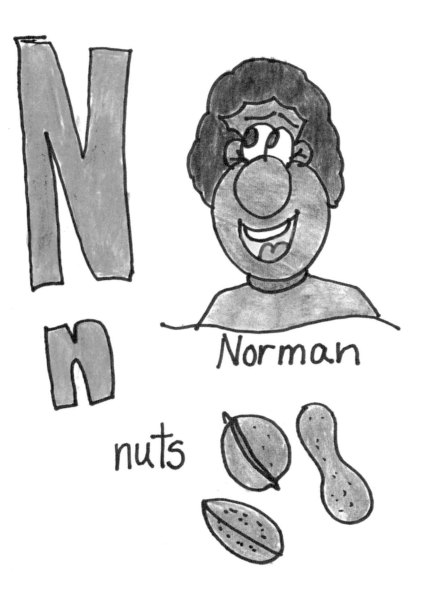

Oo

O o

Olivia

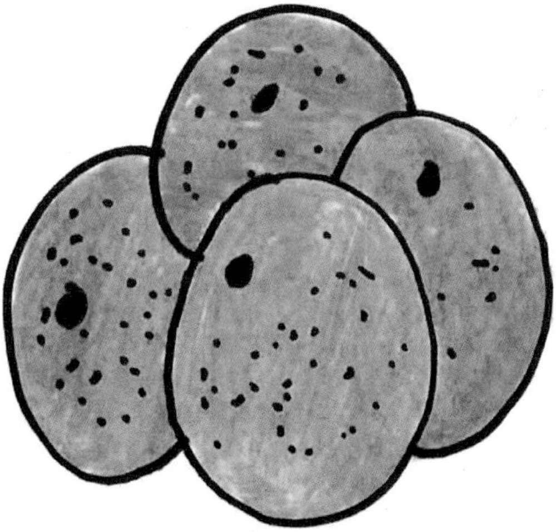

Oranges

Pp

P

p

Peter

pan

Qq

Q q

Quincy

quilt

Rr

R r

Rachel

roses

Ss

S s

Samuel

snake

Tt

T

Thomas

t

Tomatoes

Uu

U u

Uzziah

umbrellas

Vv

V v

Vanessa

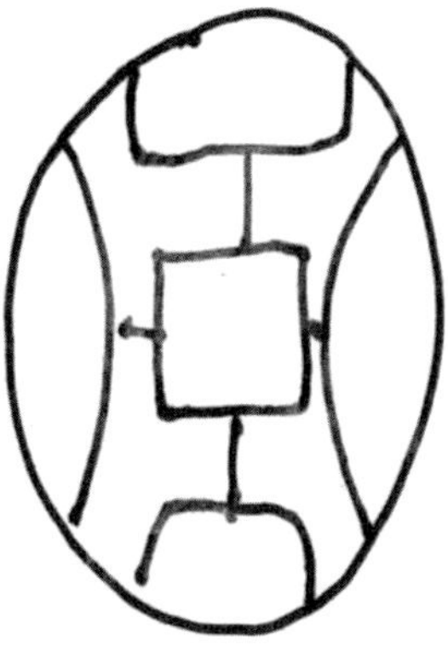

Volleyball

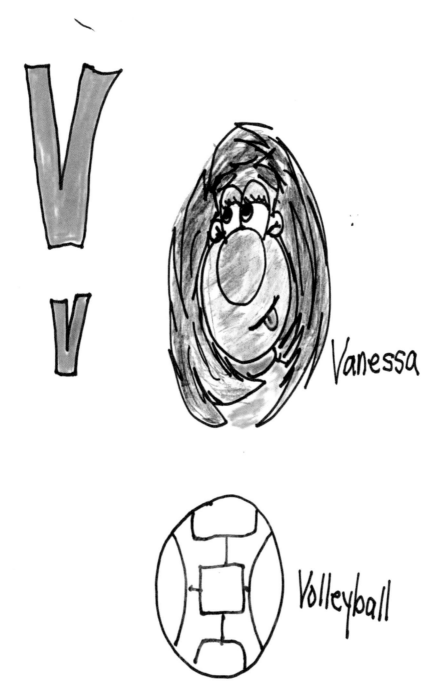

Ww

W w

Winnie

Watermelon

Xx

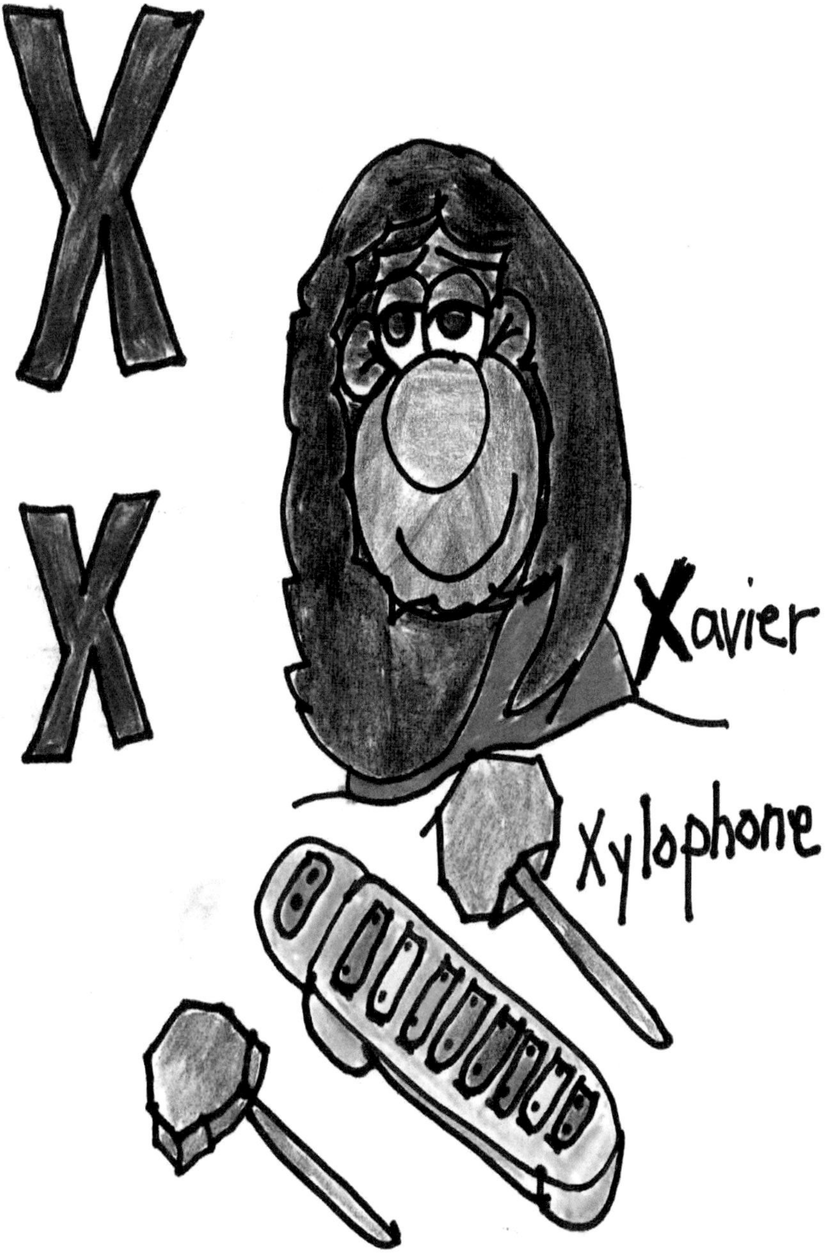
X x
Xavier
Xylophone

Yy

Y

Yen

y

Yarn

Zz

Z z

Zabella

The End

Made in the USA
Monee, IL
04 May 2022

95131284R00033